LEARNING WHAT SCARES YOU

Collective rethinking; creating community of lifelong learners

By

John Newton

TABLE OF CONTENTS

INTRODUCTION

Even if there is little evidence to support our ideas, we nevertheless dispute and fight over them. We must learn to challenge and change our beliefs as well as better comprehend their nature and how they are created.

We are divided along ethnic, political, religious, and moral lines. Our convictions, which are often on an extremely unstable basis, are what cause our division.

Individually, we are far less knowledgeable than we believe. Most of our perceptions are illusions.

We are not the intelligent beings we believe ourselves to be. We must learn how to reflect on, challenge, and improve our views if we are to participate in more sensible dialogues.

It is essential to have a thorough grasp of how our beliefs are formed and function.

Other than the opinions of individuals we love and trust, we have no proof at all for some of our most fundamental beliefs.

The certainty we feel in our views is absurd given how little we know, yet it is also crucial.

CHAPTER ONE

REEVALUATING OUR VIEWS

Most of us want to live in a better society, but we all have different views, values, morals, and strategies for achieving that goal. • Until there is compelling proof to the contrary, assume that most individuals are behaving in good faith.

• Start discussing our views and how we came to have them with one another.

• Gain a deeper understanding of our own and other people's thought processes.

• Show greater tolerance for competing viewpoints, even those that appear extreme.

To do this, a conversation is essential. We will continue to see one another as adversaries and engage in conflict if we are unable to communicate.

It may seem tough to have conversations across differences, yet it is feasible. However, there are a few prerequisites to having dialogues that could seem pointless or even impossible.

We must first acknowledge and accept that our views have not been created via a deliberative process of evidence assessment. Most topics, particularly complicated social ones, need us to recognize our ignorance and be willing to change our minds.

It follows that we should have a conversation since it is absurd for us to assume the worst of one another or to be adversaries.

The prerequisites are as follows:

1. Be willing to examine and update our views. Our beliefs are precariously rooted.

2. Stop seeing one another as rivals. We cannot be adversaries. There can be no discourse if we are adversaries.

3. Be ready to converse with those we disagree with. We must understand that communication is the only path to success. No progress can be achieved if a person is hostile, threatening, or silent.

4. Be prepared to put your confidence in one another and act in good faith. Regardless of how the talk turns out, to be genuine, impartial, open-minded, and honest.

5. Have the ability to appreciate one another and one another's opinions. must understand

that having respect is not the same as just displaying respect.

6. Be prepared to follow certain ground rules. covenants in conversation, both to make and use.

7. Be prepared to learn how to have impossible talks.

People are ecstatic when others change their minds about something, but they lack the will to do the same for themselves.

This ad campaign's tagline, "Think Different," was introduced with a quotation from Apple Inc. You may create habits that help you succeed in both your personal and professional lives when you learn to "think differently."

"The individuals who are insane enough to believe they can change the world are the ones who do," the advertisement's last sentence reads.

Are you prepared for your life to alter in that way? So let's get going.

CHAPTER TWO

"Think Different"

You can only achieve what you have already accomplished if you continue to do what you have been doing. One way to define thinking differently is to introduce fresh concepts in place of old ones. Your attitude, your neighborhood, or the whole planet may be challenged by these concepts.

You don't only engage in alternative thinking when you need inspiration. Instead, it's a regular, subconscious habit that has an impact on many aspects of your life.

Making diverse methods of thinking a habit

Here are five strategies to start thinking differently and alter your present frame of mind.

1. Retrain your mind to think positively.

While having negative thoughts is a normal aspect of being human, your goals shouldn't be hampered by them.

Negative thoughts are linked by psychologists to a variety of mental health conditions, such as:

- Depression
- Anxiety
- Constant concern
- Compulsive behavior disorder

These thinking patterns sap your drive and implant the notion that you are unworthy in your mind. While being positive is a wonderful thing, it may be harmful to cover up your negative ideas.

Instead, substitute reasonable expectations for your negative ideas. Say, for instance, "I will do my best to accomplish this, and if I fail, I can always try again until I succeed," rather than "I can't do this" or "I can do this."

Possessing a realistic outlook offers you the ability to rise to obstacles and develop resilience. Making this style of thinking a habit may be accomplished by developing a mantra, such as "I am enough," that you repeat each day.

General Health

"My brain is quite sharp. I have a healthy physique. My soul is at peace.

Mind

I design my route and joyfully follow it.

I reach new heights thanks to my optimistic beliefs.

"Every day, I am overcoming my worries and becoming stronger."

"Since I have a choice, I'll have a nice day."

"I don't mind being proven incorrect,"

2. Do not be hesitant to inquire

Students make the finest leaders. Therefore, if you want to be a leader in your field, start by asking questions that will both broaden your knowledge of the world and inspire you to approach your work in novel ways.

- How does it function?
- How can I make it better?
- Why do people think and behave the way they do?

New ideas are paved by an inquisitive mind.

Uncertain about where to begin? Simply go with your instincts. For instance, don't be hesitant to ask inquiries if anything about the setting doesn't seem right.

3. Consider issues from several angles

You must be open to taking into account other viewpoints if you wish to approach an issue differently. If you've ever seen a Monet painting, for instance, you know that you need to step back to appreciate the work. If you go too near to his paintings, they transform from gentle landscapes to streaks of color on a canvas.

Sometimes our proximity to or distance from an idea prevents us from thinking effectively. Consider the notion in the context of a larger picture to avoid being in the same rut. Explore your possibilities after zooming in on the idea's smaller features.

Even shutting off your brain might aid in clear thinking. Your mind starts to unwind, for instance, when you take a shower or are drifting off to sleep. These circumstances may inspire fresh or original thoughts.

Don't save all of your creative thinking for when you are sitting at a desk. Another technique to stimulate your creativity is exercise. Studies have shown that exercises like jogging, swimming, or walking improve cognitive functions.

Being open-minded makes it easier to consider all the potential solutions to an issue.

4. Dream big.

Martin Luther King, Jr. is a perfect illustration of a distinct way of thinking. He was a visionary who pursued his interests and broke away from prevailing ideologies to imagine a better future.

Every excellent leader has a dream that is founded on their interests. These aspirations don't have to be realistic. They may defy societal conventions or be unlike anything you have ever attempted. (Even if it means taking chances and eschewing the security of predictability.)

Sometimes, you may not live to see your desire come true. You're not a failure, despite this, of course. Instead, set more manageable objectives along the road as stepping stones.

For instance, if you want to run a marathon, don't just sign up for the lengthy event without any preparation. You may not succeed if you tried. Every mile you run, however, is a victory and gets you closer to your eventual objective if you start by working up to 26.2 miles one mile at a time.

Small victories along the road will encourage you to keep going.

5. Provide personal comments to yourself.

Not every suggestion you make will work. You'll err from time to time, and that's OK. Making mistakes helps you learn from them, making your subsequent ideas stronger.

Every choice you make and every original thought you have should be accompanied by feedback. Consider the idea's benefits and drawbacks. Before moving through with the concept, you may also consult with trustworthy pals.

How to change your way of thinking in life

The mind is like a muscle. Like all of your muscles, it will become stronger the more you use it. Therefore, it will be simpler the more you practice diverse ways of thinking. The five methods for thinking creatively will eventually become second nature to you. It will just develop normally.

CHAPTER THREE

Unlearning and Relearning

People may prosper and progress when they have the bravery to admit their knowledge gaps, the desire to widen their viewpoints, and the ability to accept changes. Situations in the world often force individuals to learn, unlearn, and relearn. Take into account the pressures exerted on people to modify their working methods during the COVID-19 epidemic. Office employees had to quickly become used to online collaboration and workflow management technologies, while nurses had to retrain how to do telehealth patient assessments.

People may succeed in a continuously changing environment by adapting to changes quickly and with an open mind.

Adopting a process of learning, unlearning, and relearning is necessary for this.

What Is the Cycle of Learning, Unlearning, and Reinforcement?

Many individuals are used to studying by gathering knowledge and piling facts on top of one another. This strategy has advantages, but it also has drawbacks. It may not always take into consideration the need to modify when new technologies, practices, and attitudes manifest themselves.

On the other hand, the cycle of learning, unlearning and relearning necessitates that individuals review and assess the applicability of previously acquired knowledge when new information becomes accessible. People may need to get rid of old ideas and reorganize their mental models as a result of these analyses.

Unlearning Information and methods of operation

People often have to unlearn facts and behaviors to learn new ones. Even something as simple as formatting a page could need unlearning a procedure when a word processor update changes the user interface. Or, new research can reveal conclusions that conflict with long-held assumptions, necessitating a full reorganization of a profession's established methods.

For instance, a recent study discovered that approximately 400 common medical procedures conflict with findings reported in prestigious medical publications. Healthcare personnel needs to relearn what was formerly thought to be common knowledge about anything from how to handle pain in emergency rooms to when to operate on a patient's knee for a torn meniscus to be in line with current research.

Knowledge Reconception in the Light of New Information

Reconceiving previous knowledge in the light of fresh information is necessary to move ahead and avoid being trapped in what has become outdated. This requires questioning preconceived notions and creating room for knowledge that may not comport with one's current mental model.

For instance, many corporate executives long believed that productivity would suffer as well as cooperation and control would be lost as a consequence of working remotely.

However, after the epidemic, organizational leaders that are prepared to reconsider such notions will have a better chance of success in the post-COVID-19 period, when worker expectations have drastically changed.

In a recent Prudential study of American employees, over half of the respondents claimed they would quit their present positions if their employers stopped allowing remote work. Additionally, several polls conducted after the pandemic show that a sizable proportion of CEOs have discovered that remote work boosts worker productivity. These illustrations highlight how critical it is to modify mental models to keep pace with changing circumstances.

The Value of the Model of Learning, Unlearning, and Relearning

Adopting the learning, unlearning, and relearning approach is essential if one wants to remain current in their area. It is fundamentally necessary given the speed of change in almost every industry, including business, IT, and healthcare. New technologies like automation and artificial intelligence are changing the nature of employment and rendering obsolete formerly effective skills.

As a consequence, many occupations that were there only a few decades ago no longer exist, and more ones will probably vanish in the next years. On the other hand, new occupations that need new knowledge and skill sets are starting to appear. A 2020 World Economic Forum research predicts that many people would need to pick up new skill sets and knowledge to continue doing their existing jobs successfully in the years to come, in addition to a significant number of new professions needing new abilities.

However, upskilling and reskilling may provide workers the ability to find their place in evolving workplaces. As older occupations are lost or modified, learning new skills enables people to do new tasks. For instance, the need for phone receptionists can be obsolete thanks to an automated system. Retraining, however, may enable such receptionists to move to other roles within their businesses and keep their jobs.

Learning new skills to improve one's performance in their existing position or adapt to changes in their sector also contributes to work success and stability.

Professionals in marketing, for instance, would probably benefit from acquiring training in data analytics to improve their usefulness in an area where the importance of data has grown.

CHAPTER FOUR

The Learning, Unlearning, and Relearning Model: Embracing Strategies

What are the requirements for effectively adopting the learning, unlearning, and relearning model? To start, this paradigm does not entail losing information. Instead, it necessitates rejecting default assumptions and considering one's beliefs, decisions, and methods of action.

The following advice may assist people in adopting this flexible method of learning.

Identify and Combat Your Confirmation Bias

People naturally have the propensity to seek out or interpret data that supports their own opinions. They are often less receptive to learning new concepts and methods of operation that contradict their preconceptions as a result of this confirmation bias. Individuals must, however, analyze and reconsider their ideas and methods of operation to learn, unlearn, and relearn.

People may focus on being aware of their confirmation bias to enhance their capacity to adopt this learning technique. They may then look for viewpoints that vary from their own. By acquiring knowledge from many sources and engaging in discussion with individuals from other backgrounds, one may also combat confirmation bias.

Become growth-minded

People who think they can improve their skills via hard effort, thoughtful decision-making, and constructive criticism may do more than those who believe skills are just natural. People that have a development mindset are more inclined to try out novel approaches, learn from their failures, and ask for feedback.

The learning, unlearning, and relearning paradigm is supported by each of these actions. By encouraging their curiosity, individuals may cultivate a growth mentality. This entails exchanging one's guilt or anxiety about ignorance for awe and joy at the many chances for learning and discovery that exist.

Pose more questions

People's interactions and mental processes take on new dimensions as additional questions are asked. Additionally, it aids in learning new facts and broadens one's perspective. The use of questions is crucial for deeper learning. The questions that people choose to ask or refrain from asking often influence how much they can learn, unlearn, and relearn.

Keep an eye out for shifting industry trends

When determining what to learn, unlearn, and relearn, people must use strategy. Their decisions should be in line with clear objectives like professional or personal development. A person may obtain important insights about what new skills they need to master, which communication techniques they need to unlearn, and which techniques they need to relearn by keeping up with shifting trends in their business, for instance.

Individuals may stay up with new technology and advances in their areas by reading industry magazines, joining networking groups on LinkedIn and other platforms, and attending professional conferences.

Further Your Education Retooling one's skill set is a fantastic opportunity provided by education. A professional certificate in cybersecurity or an advanced nursing degree may assist individuals to become ready for the most recent job needs in their respective industries.

People who are returning to school have many chances to reskill and upskill thanks to well-thought-out courses and teaching from industry professionals. This may assist professionals in developing the skills necessary to remain current in their industry or in making successful career moves.

www.ingramcontent.com/pod-product-compliance
Lightning Source LLC
LaVergne TN
LVHW052111160826
845678LV00015B/3494
9798370696251